THIS JOURNAL BELONGS TO:

CW01091251

#ME

DISCLAIMER

Copyright 2022 Oliver Drakeford | My People Patterns. All Rights Reserved.

No part of this publication may be reproduced, stored in a retrieval system or transmitted in any form or by any means, electronic, mechanical, photocopying, recording, scanning or otherwise, except as permitted under Sections 107 or 108 of the 1976 United States Copyright Act, without the prior written permission of the Publisher. Requests to the Publisher for permission should be directed to www.MyPeoplePatterns.com.

The Publisher and the author make no representations or warranties with respect to the accuracy or completeness of the contents of this work and specifically disclaim all warranties, including without limitation warranties of fitness for a particular purpose. No warranty may be created or extended by sales or promotional materials.

The advice and strategies contained herein may not be suitable for every situation. This work is sold with the understanding that the publisher is not engaged in rendering medical, legal, or other professional advice or services. If professional assistance is required, the services of a competent professional person should be sought. Neither the Publisher nor the author shall be liable for damages arising therefrom.

The fact that an individual, organization or website is referred to in this work as a citation and/or potential source of further information does not mean that the author or the Publisher endorses the information the individual, organization or website may provide or recommendations they/it may make. Further, readers should be aware that Internet websites listed in this work may have changed since date of publication.

THE FREE COMPANION COURSE FOR PARENTS, CAREGIVERS, AND ADULTS

F.O.R.T.ified Relationships
THE FREE ONLINE COMPANION COURSE FOR PARENTS & CAREGIVERS

Thank you for looking at this book for the special teenager in your life, I've made sure to fill it with practical tools, skills, and techniques that I hope will set them up for the years ahead.

I would like to invite you to take advantage of the free companion course that accompanies this book, designed for adults. This course is totally free, and all you need to do is sign up for it using the link below.

As a psychotherapist specializing in family work, and after running a residential treatment center for teens for the last few years, I have come to believe that parents and caregivers need to be supported as much as adolescents. This online course is a way to provide you with some of the insights and education I've shared with hundreds of families over the course of my career.

Oliver Drakeford, LMFT, CGP
Licensed Marriage & Family Therapist #104987

www.MyPeoplePatterns.com/fortified

FREE COURSE FOR ADULTS AND PARENTS OF TEENS

FOR CLINICIANS
OR POST-IT NOTE FANS

POST-IT NOTE TEMPLATE

The tools in this journal and workbook are conveniently shaped to fit on a Post-It Note. In some of the videos on the My People Pattern's YouTube Channel, you will be able to see this and learn how to print them. The link below will take you to a PDF containing a template that has all of the tools on it.

THE TOOLS YOU
CAN PRINT ON
POST-IT NOTES

DEDICATION

Finn, Asa, Evelyn & Bertie.

Peter J Hume.
Table Two.
Rosa, Sarah, Neil & Huevo.
Victoria, Carrie & Keaton.
Ange & Lyndsay.
Chelsea, Nicky, Michael.
Derek, Andrea, Alexa, Ricky, and Sam.
Cindy & Leanne.
Steve Keith.
My Parents

COVER- Selma_Lou at Fiverr.
GOGO - tasartir at Fiverr

ABOUT

Like many people in North America, I rescued GoGo, my first dog, during the COVID-19 pandemic. During the first few months of getting accustomed to having a dog in my life, I did not expect how much I would learn about myself and the nature of relationships in general.

Our daily walks around my neighborhood gave me time away from my therapy sessions, during which my mind would slow down. There were days when a parallel process seemed to be happening, and I'd observe behaviors in myself or GoGo that made me think of a problem I was helping a client with.

Over the course of a year, these interactions, observations, and stories I'd note about him would weave their way into my clinical work. Most often, they were stories that let me introduce a topic relevant to the client, and other times it was a metaphor I would use to engage families in a discussion. The teenagers I worked with most noticeably seemed to have more buy-in to the session when I started with a story about my dog. This was the start of My People Patterns, the YouTube Channel and Instagram page, and our mission is to help grow great relationships with ourselves, others, and our family.

Hit follow, and say hi!

Oliver & GoGo

LEARN MORE HERE

PS - if GoGo and I have a video explaining a topic more, look for him on the page, and there will be a link that takes you to the clip.

@MyPeoplePatterns

INTRODUCTION

This journal and workbook is divided into 52 sections, one for each week of the year. The weeks are undated so it can be started at any time. Each of the 52 sections has a tool or a skill in the form of an acronym, along with thought-provoking questions designed to develop insight and introspection.

52 TOOLS & SKILLS

Each of the 52 sections contains a therapeutic tool, helpful skill, or motivational aid in the form of an acronym, along with an explanation of it. Some of these skills are tools are not taught in schools and have to be discovered later in life, often in therapy or out of necessity.

QUESTIONS

Asking the right questions at the right time can change our ideas of who we are and how we see the world around us in a process known as introspection. As a psychotherapist, I've seen clients have profound transformations due to looking inside themselves and shining some light on who they are and what they believe in.

ACRONYMS

In studies, using acronyms as a method of remembering information is consistently associated with higher performance in studies and an increase in motivation. In everyday life, acronyms are an easy and fun way to retain information and tool that can help us.

JOURNALING

A vast and growing body of research shows how writing can be used therapeutically to address issues ranging from grief to trauma and everything in between. Writing by hand has been shown in studies to stimulate the same parts of our brain that are activated in meditation, which may improve or increase creativity. Other studies using MRIs have shown that sequential hand movements used while writing can activate large regions of the brain responsible for thinking, language, healing, and working memory.

TOPICS AND THEMES

MOTIVATION

BIG FEELINGS

FRIENDS

SUCCESS

STUCK

ANXIETY

SELF

CONFLICT

HOW THIS WORKS

"Low self-esteem is like driving through life with your handbrake on."
Maxwell Maltz

#FLY

SELF

FIRST

LOVE

YOURSELF

QUOTE
RELATED QUOTE AND INSPIRATIONAL WORDS

WEEKLY TOOL OR SKILL
EACH WEEK HAS A TOOL OR SKILL IN THE FORM OF AN EASILY REMEMBERED ACRONYM

EXPLANATION OR EXERCISE
THIS IS WHERE TO TOOL IS EXPLAINED OR MORE DETAILS ARE GIVEN

Self-love, self-care, and self-esteem are all t̶e̶r̶m̶s̶ ̶w̶e̶'̶v̶e̶ ̶heard, but d̶o̶ you know that there are three parts to loving y̶o̶u̶r̶s̶e̶lf that we should all be aware of:

1. **Self-Esteem -** this part is about how much you respect yourself and the confidence you have in your own abilities and unique talents. Self-esteem help us feel more confident and develops our self-respect.

2. **Inner Critic -** We all have an inner critic that reminds us what's good and what's bad. When this voice is too loud or too harsh, it can lead to feelings of depression and anxiety. Turning this voice down and keeping it in check is a important part of self-love.

3. **Self-Acceptance -** the last part of self-love is that you can accept yourself a you are, at the same time as wanting to improve or be the best version of you.

HOW
THIS
WORKS

WEEKLY REFLECTION

THESE QUESTIONS HELP US FOCUS ON THE WEEK AHEAD TO SET INTENTIONS. OR THEY HELP US REFLECT ON THE PREVIOUS WEEK TO CELEBRATE SUCCESS OR LEARN FROM MISTAKES

WEEKLY

LEARN What did I learn about myself this week?

PRIDE What do I feel good about doing or accomplishing this week?

CURIOUS What topics or areas do I find myself curious about knowing more about

PRIORITIES FOR THIS WEEK:

In what ways do you show love for yourself?
What could you do more of?

When was the last time you told yourself how awesome you are? What gets in the way of that?

PLANNING & PRIORITIES

ORGANIZING YOUR PRIORITIES FOR THE WEEK IS A KEY COMPONENT OF PRODUCTIVITY.

DEEP DIVE

THE QUESTIONS IN THIS SECTION ARE A DEEPER DIVE INTO WHO YOU ARE, AND HELP YOU REFLECT ON YOUR SELF, IDENTITY, AND FUTURE.

THE WEEKLY REFLECTION QUESTIONS

MOTIVATION

GOAL What are my goals for this week?

BLOCKS What is it about me that gets in the way of me reaching my goals?

VISION What could I do differently when and if I run into my blocks?

BIG FEELINGS

WIN What were the big wins for you from the previous week?

GROWTH What is your growth edge or areas that you could do better in?

GOAL What are the main goals of the week ahead?

SOCIAL

MORE What do I need more help with or more of this week?

PRIDE What could I do this week that will make me feel proud?

HAPPY Who do I feel grateful for this week, and why?

STUCK

WHO Who can I help this week?

WHAT What are three things I can do this week to move forward?

HELP Who is the ideal person to help me if I am stuck?

These questions are shorter and designed to be asked at the beginning of each week. They either focus your thoughts on the week ahead or encourage healthy reflection and growth from the previous week.

ANXIETY

HAPPY   What are y grateful for the most this week?

INTENT   What is my personal intention this week?

MINDFUL   In what areas can I be more mindful in?

SELF

LEARN   What did I learn about myself this week?

PRIDE   What do I feel good about doing or accomplishing this week?

CURIOUS   What topics or areas do I find myself curious about ?

CONFLICT

WHO   Which of my relationships, if any, should I look to improve?

HOW   Can I do or say anything different around this person

SHIFT   What is one thing I like about someone I have difficulty with?

SUCCESS

AWESOME   What totally lit me up and excited me last week?

CONTENT   What am I satisfied with just the way it is?

GROWTH   In what area should I focus on improving in this week?

THE JOURNAL

"**Low self-esteem is like driving through life with your handbrake on.**"
Maxwell Maltz

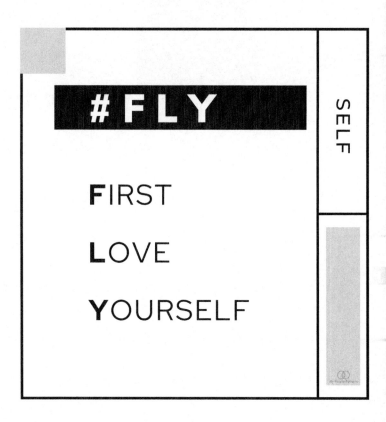

#FLY

FIRST

LOVE

YOURSELF

SELF

Self-love, self-care, and self-esteem are all terms we've heard, but did you know that there are three parts to loving yourself that we should all be aware of?

1. **Self-Esteem** - this part is about how much you respect yourself and the confidence you have in your abilities and unique talents. Self-esteem helps us feel more confident and develops our self-respect.
2. **Inner Critic -** We all have an inner critic that reminds us what's good and what's bad. When this voice is too loud or too harsh, it can lead to feelings of depression and anxiety. Turning this voice down and keeping it in check is an important part of self-love.
3. **Self-Acceptance** - the last part of self-love is that you can accept yourself as you are while simultaneously wanting to improve or be the best version of yourself.

WEEKLY

LEARN   What did I learn about myself this week?

PRIDE   What do I feel good about doing or accomplishing this week?

CURIOUS   What topics or areas do I find myself curious about knowing more of?

LEARN

PRIDE

CURIOUS

PRIORITIES FOR THIS WEEK:

In what ways do you *show* love for yourself?
What could you do more of?

#FLY

What are the top five qualities your friends and family would say that you have?

#HATERS

HAVING

ANGER

TOWARDS

EVERYONE

REACHING

SUCCESS

There's a lot of truth about the **#HATERS** acronym, often, people express hatred towards those they are jealous of, and success is one thing that is guaranteed to spark some envy. This is what therapists call 'projection.' Here are some ways of thinking about **#HATERS.**

GROWTH - shaking off an attack from someone who's jealous of you is tough at the best of times, but if you are able to avoid it getting to you, then you might be able to grow from the experience.

INDICATORS In a weird way, if you're getting the attention of people who are envious of you, it means you're doing something right.

COMPASSION - If you can muster up some compassion for those attacking you, you're doing an outstanding job and are likely reaching Oprah-like levels of enlightenment. You will also be doing good if you don't take the bait and engage with them.

LEARN MORE
ABOUT
PROJECTION HERE

WEEKLY

WHO	Which of my relationships, if any, should I look to improve?
HOW	Can I do or say anything different around this person?
SHIFT	What is one thing I like or admire about someone I have difficulty with?

WIN

GROWTH

GOAL

PRIORITIES FOR THIS WEEK:

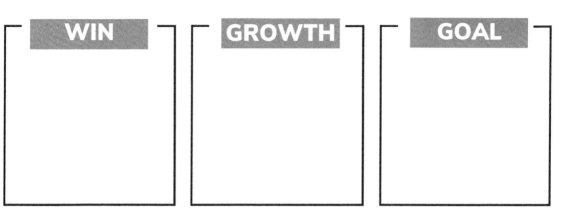

What sort of things have made you envious recently?

#HATERS

What do the things you get envious of say about you?

#STIC

Stop

Take a breath

Imagine Consequences

Choose

#STIC is an acronym developed by Steven Saul as part of a Mindfulness-Based Program for Adolescents and is designed to help teens who sometimes make impulsive decisions. We all make hasty decisions once in a while, sometimes, there are no consequences, and other times we regret not thinking things through before acting on an idea or feeling. This tool is a reminder to CHOOSE rather than react.

STOP - rather than react to a feeling or thought, try and recognize that you are being activated by something.

TAKE A BREATH - to slow thoughts and behaviors down and try to understand what's happening.

IMAGINE FUTURE CONSEQUENCES - if you can remember or imagine what the consequences of what you're about to do are, you can change the direction you're headed in, mainly if those consequences are negative.

CHOOSE - We might not have much choice in our feelings, but there is always a choice in our behaviors. If you know what the consequences will be or might be, choose wisely.

WEEKLY

WIN   What were the big wins for you from the previous week?

GROWTH   What is your growth edge– these are areas that you could do better in?

GOAL   What are the main goals of the week ahead?

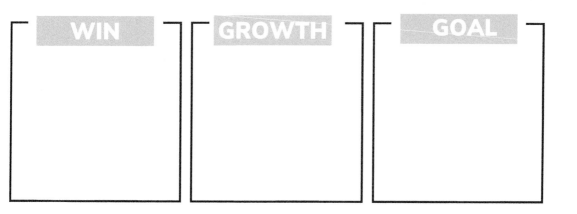

WIN

GROWTH

GOAL

PRIORITIES FOR THIS WEEK:

Do you agree or disagree that there is always a choice in our behaviors?

#STIC

Is there an event or incident you can recall in which you acted impulsively and regretted the behaviors? What would you have done differently?

#SMILE

SEE

MIRACLES

IN

LIVE

EVERY DAY

Are you a glass-half-full type, or are you a glass-half-empty type? There's a social psychology experiment I love that studied people with both mindsets, and the results were fascinating.

In the study, those with a more positive outlook on life literally saw things in a different way from those with a negative mindset. The 'glass-half-full' volunteers found a $10 note on the floor that had been deliberately left by the psychologists as part of the experiment. Whereas the glass-half-empty group didn't see the note when they walked past, even though it was in the same place.

Our attitude changes the way we see the world.

Watch the Video on Mindset by My People Patterns here:

WEEKLY

GOAL   What are my goals for this week?

BLOCKS   What is it about me that gets in the way of me reaching my goals?

VISION   What could I do differently when and if I run into my blocks

GOAL

BLOCK

VISION

PRIORITIES FOR THIS WEEK:

Are you a glass-half-empty kind of person, or more of a glass-half-full type? Would you change it if you could?

#SMILE

What do you imagine would be different in your life if you actively looked for positive things each day?
How might you do this?

#WOOP

WISH

OUTCOME

OBSTACLE

PLAN

If you have goals for your future or dreams of what it's going to be like in a few years, you need to know **#WOOP**! This is a tool that is easy to use and scientifically proven to work.

WISH - decide on a goal you would like to accomplish sometime in the next three months. Make it realistic and achievable, so 'winning the lottery is probably not going to work, but 'getting an A in Chemistry, might be more practical.

OUTCOME - envision the best possible outcome that would result from accomplishing this goal. Get into detail about what it would feel like and be like.

OBSTACLES - what are the obstacles within you that get in the way? Procrastination? Anxiety?

PLAN - Create a plan for overcoming your obstacles, and get clear on what you would do if this happens again. Use an IF/WHEN ..... THEN format.
ie *If* I get nervous, *then* I will use my deep breathing tool.

Watch the Video on #WOOP
from My People Patterns here

WEEKLY

AWESOME What totally lit me up and excited me?

CONTENT What am I satisfied with just the way it is?

GROWTH In what area should I focus on improving in this week?

AWESOME

CONTENT

GROWTH

PRIORITIES FOR THIS WEEK:

What's a goal or wish you have that is realistic and achievable in the next two or three months? Describe in detail especially any feelings that come up.

#WOOP

What are some of the internal obstacles that might come up for you while working towards this goal? What could you do about them if / when they show up?

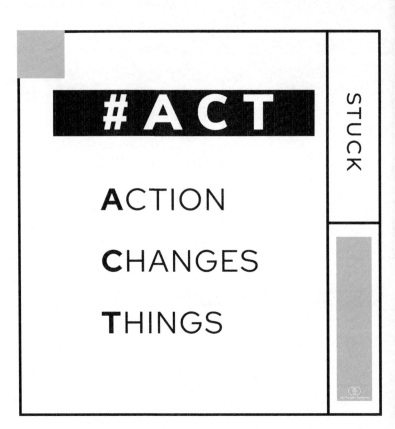

#ACT

ACTION

CHANGES

THINGS

STUCK

Sometimes when we are stuck, it is due to a state of mind known as ambivalence. This is a mixture of feelings, often opposing feelings, like wanting to stay in bed but also knowing you need to go to school or work. As a species, we humans tend to avoid things we don't understand or find confusing, like, quantum physics or ... ambivalence.

As a result of avoiding ambivalence, we never take the opportunity to think through these feelings and sort them out, so we remain stuck for much longer than is truly necessary. It would be like hitting snooze on your alarm *all day* - the only reason this doesn't happen is we eventually address our ambivalence of getting out of bed and lean into the idea that perhaps we should go to school.

Sometimes getting unstuck is about leaning into our ambivalence rather than avoiding it.

Watch the Video on ambivalence from My People Patterns here

WEEKLY

WHO Who can I help this week?

WHAT What are three things I can do this week to move forward?

HELP Who is the ideal person to help me if I am stuck?

WHO

WHAT

HELP

PRIORITIES FOR THIS WEEK:

How do you react to failure or disappointment?
Do you think you have any choice in your reactions?

A C T

How often do you talk yourself out of taking action or doing
one small thing that moves you closer to your goals?

#STRESS

SOMEONE

TRYING TO

REPAIR

EVERY

SITUATION

SOLO

This acronym might be for you if you identify as a people pleaser. Many people try to help or rescue others from their problems by taking on extra responsibilities or doing more for them to the point where they feel stressed, anxious, or burned out. Maybe these are familiar:

- We try and help or fix other people's problems out of kindness
- We agree to do something we really don't want to or can't do
- We try and make sure everyone is OK
- We struggle to ask for help ourselves
- We tend to speak on behalf of someone, even when they can do so without you.

Watch the Video on People Pleasing from My People Patterns here

WEEKLY

HAPPY   What am I grateful for the most this week?

INTENT   What is my personal intention this week?

MINDFUL   In what areas can I be more mindful in?

HAPPY

INTENT

MINDFUL

PRIORITIES FOR THIS WEEK:

Under what circumstances are you more likely to over-extend yourself by helping other people?

STRESS

What would it be like if you were to be slightly *less* responsible for other people, and slightly *more* responsible for yourself?

#LOVE

LISTEN

OVERLOOK

VALUE

ENCOURAGE

FRIENDS

When it comes to familial, romantic, and platonic relationships, the word 'LOVE' is used a lot. While it might mean different things to different people, it's necessary sometimes to remember that love is a verb - it's a doing word. This means we sometimes have to do things to show that we love someone.

This *can* be as simple as saying 'I love you,' but actually, we feel loved by others when they show it as well as say it. This acronym for **#LOVE** reminds us of some ways we can actively show our love for the special people in our lives.

LISTEN - to hear, not to respond
OVERLOOK - mistakes or petty incidents
VALUE - we look after things we value, and that includes people
ENCOURAGE - support and encouragement is an often overlooked way to express care for someone.

WEEKLY

MORE   What do I need more help with or more of this week?

PRIDE   What could I do this week that will make me feel proud?

HAPPY   Who do I feel grateful for this week, and why?

MORE

PRIDE

HAPPY

PRIORITIES FOR THIS WEEK:

Write about the time you felt the most loved. Who was there and how did you experience it as love?

L O V E

How do you express your love to people you're fond of? Hint: Think about the Five Love Languages of Words, Deeds, Touch, Action or Time.

#TEAM

Together

Everyone

Achieves

More

My People Patterns

Teamwork is the ability to work with others towards a common goal, and in doing so, the team can achieve more than just one person. While it's not always possible to do homework or work on projects as a team, there is a way to put together a group of people who support you and who could provide input to your life and your personal growth journey. This is sometimes called your *Soul Tribe*.

> **"1+1>2"**
> - Unknown

WEEKLY

GOAL What are my goals for this week?

BLOCKS What is it about me that gets in the way of me reaching my goals?

VISION What could I do differently when and if I run into my blocks?

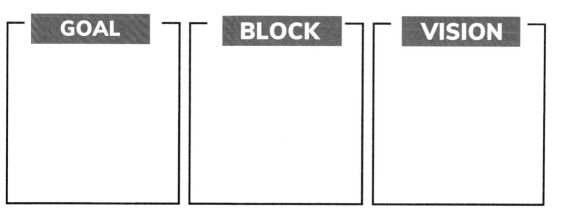

GOAL

BLOCK

VISION

PRIORITIES FOR THIS WEEK:

Who are the people in your life that you are closest to? Who is the easiest to connect with and why?

#TEAM

Who do you trust the most and why? Who encourages you the most? Who could you turn to for advice?

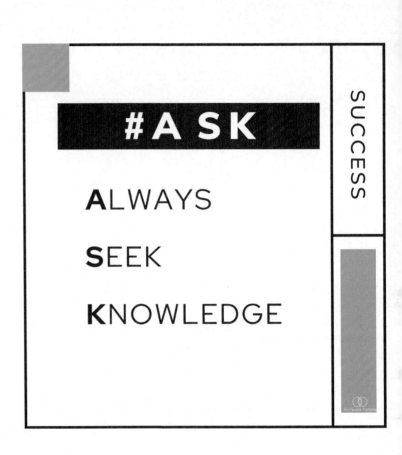

 # A S K

ALWAYS

SEEK

KNOWLEDGE

SUCCESS

For most of life's problems, we seek help from a specialist – when you're sick, you see a doctor, and if your tooth hurts, you go to the dentist. For some reason, we're a bit more reserved when it comes to personal growth or happiness.

Some of our tips to get better at asking for help

1. Be precise in what you are asking for.
2. Ask at the right time, in the right way.
3. Don't make assumptions as to what someone does or doesn't know.
4. Be open to helping others to set the tone of helpfulness.

WEEKLY

AWESOME   What totally lit me up and excited me?

CONTENT   What am I satisfied with just the way it is?

GROWTH   In what area should I focus on improving in this week?

AWESOME

CONTENT

GROWTH

PRIORITIES FOR THIS WEEK:

Do you find it difficult to ask for help in certain areas?

#ASK

Which fits you better and why? "If I ask for help, I might seem weak", OR "If I ask for help, I might be burdening the other person"

#DEARMAN

DESCRIBE

EXPRESS

ASSERT

REINFORCE

MINDFUL

APPEARANCE

NEGOTIATE

The acronym **#DEARMAN** is a Dialectical Behavioral Therapy skill used to help people communicate effectively, mainly when big feelings are going on around the topic or between two people.

DESCRIBE - this situation, using only facts (no feelings) and without judgment

EXPRESS - then express your feelings using I statements.

ASSERT - clearly state in direct terms what you want or need. Be specific.

REINFORCE - make sure you're throwing some appreciation or acknowledgment to the other person.

MINDFULNESS. - be mindful of your goal, and don't get sucked into different topics.

APPEAR CONFIDENT - show confidence, even if you don't feel it, by using eye contact and a steady tone of voice.

WEEKLY

WIN   What were the big wins for you from the previous week?

GROWTH   What is your growth edge- these are areas that you could do better in?

GOAL   What are the main goals of the week ahead?

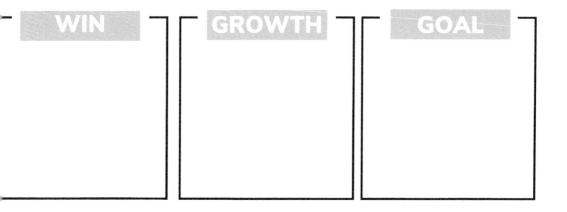

WIN

GROWTH

GOAL

PRIORITIES FOR THIS WEEK:

In what situations are you most likely to need to use this tool?

#DEARMAN

What makes it hard for you to ask for what you need or want?

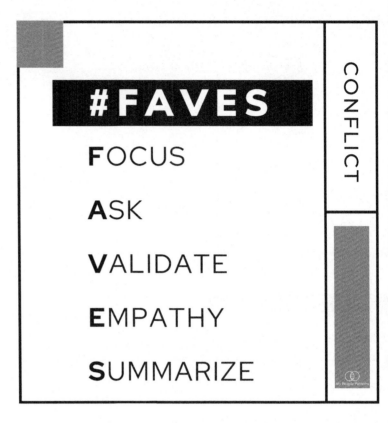

#FAVES

FOCUS

ASK

VALIDATE

EMPATHY

SUMMARIZE

CONFLICT

#FAVES is an acronym and a tool that really helps people become better communicators, specifically better listeners, and in doing so can help in difficult or tense interpersonal moments.

FOCUS	Be present, don't get distracted by chatter in your head, or by rehearsing what you're going to say next.
ASK	Asking open-ended questions helps people feel understood, particularly if the questions are expansive, meaning it gets them to talk more: "What was that like for you?"
VALIDATE	While someone is talking you can make a quick validating comment to show you are listening and acknowledging what they are saying. "Sounds like that really hurt you".
EMPATHY	"I hear you" or "I get it" is not really conveying empathy. Try to convert a richer understanding by using moe feelings words.
SUMMARIZE	To give someone the gift of being understood, summarize what they are saying in a few words. It will go a *long way*.

WEEKLY

WHO   Which of my relationships, if any, should I look to improve?

HOW   Can I do or say anything different around this person?

SHIFT   What is one thing I like or admire about someone I have difficulty with?

AWESOME

CONTENT

GROWTH

PRIORITIES FOR THIS WEEK:

What does it feel like when you're talking to someone, and you get the sense that they aren't listening to you? Who does this the most in your relationships?

#FAVES

How well do you think you listen to people and how could you improve?

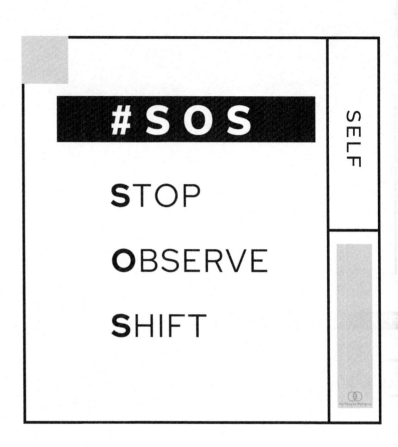

#SOS

STOP

OBSERVE

SHIFT

SELF

Negative self-talk is often at the core of our anxiety, depression, and other big feelings. It's a tough habit for some of us to kick, but it's always possible.

STOP - literally tell yourself to STOP! You may have to train yourself to *hear* your negative self-talk first, but once you catch it. Stop the pattern. It's now a choice you're making to continue.

OBSERVE -what you were saying to yourself and how it made you feel. Once you realize how detrimental it is to your well-being, it becomes easier to shift.

SHIFT- your thinking patterns. You can continue talking to yourself that way, which is familiar and what you're used to, or you could try changing the channel by focusing on other thoughts. Or you could use any of your other tools from this journal.

WEEKLY

LEARN   What did I learn about myself this week?

PRIDE   What do I feel good about doing or accomplishing this week?

CURIOUS What topics or areas do I find myself curious about knowing more of?

LEARN

PRIDE

CURIOUS

PRIORITIES FOR THIS WEEK:

What are the things you are most tough on yourself about? What triggers your negative self-talk?

#SOS

Our negative self-talk is often extremely harsh, can you re-write this in a more compassionate tone? Try using these next time you catch negative self-talk.

#W.T.F

WRITE

THE

FUTURE

My People Patterns

> "There is a vitality, a life force, an energy, a quickening that is translated through you into action, and because there is only one of you in all time, this expression is unique. And if you block it, it will never exist through any other medium and will be lost."
>
> — Martha Graham

Motivation can come and go in waves, sometimes, we are highly motivated, and other days we could not care less. If we look carefully enough, we might be able to notice what triggers and maintains our motivation, and it probably won't be the same thing for everyone. That's why asking yourself questions like the one in this workbook is essential, it will help you figure out yourself and what works for you.

WEEKLY

GOAL What are my goals for this week?

BLOCKS What is it about me that gets in the way of me reaching my goals?

VISION What could I do differently when and if I run into my blocks?

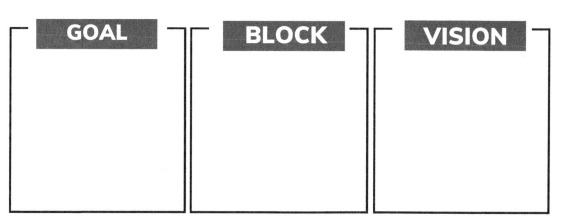

GOAL

BLOCK

VISION

PRIORITIES FOR THIS WEEK:

What matters most in your life?

W . T . F

What are you doing about the thing(s) that matter most in your life?

#HALT

HUNGRY

ANGRY

LONELY

TIRED

SELF

Whenever you feel 'off,' either anxious, spaced-out, moody, or any other state of mind that is not your normal, it's a good idea to remember to **#HALT.**

HUNGRY - this is true physiological hunger that food is going to help with. It's an annoying fact of being human that we simply cannot expect our bodies or brains to operate at full speed without nutrients and food.

ANGER / AGITATION / ANXIETY / ANNOYANCE - having any of these feelings doesn't mean anything is wrong, it just means we might not be in the best frame of mind to make decisions or be our best possible self.

LONELY -Social isolation has made us all aware of how important our relationships are, and as a species, we are wired for connection. We can still be lonely when surrounded by people, so looking at the quality of the connection is useful to restore our equilibrium.

TIRED - much like hunger, this is a physiological state that impacts our performance. Expecting ourselves to be in our normal mood or state of functioning is unrealistic if we're not getting enough rest.

WEEKLY

LEARN   What did I learn about myself this week?

PRIDE   What do I feel good about doing or accomplishing this week?

CURIOUS   What topics or areas do I find myself curious about knowing more of?

LEARN

PRIDE

CURIOUS

PRIORITIES FOR THIS WEEK:

Who has had the greatest impact on your life, and why?

#HALT

Which of the four components of H.A.L.T has the biggest impact on you most often? What can you do to change this?

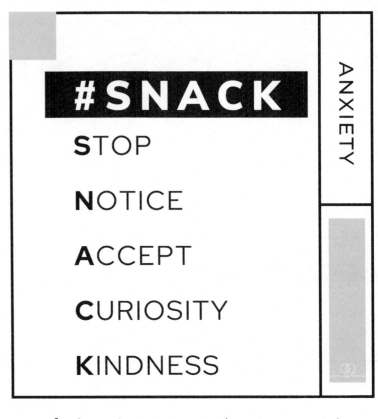

#SNACK

STOP

NOTICE

ACCEPT

CURIOSITY

KINDNESS

ANXIETY

The next time you feel anxious, stressed out, uncertain, or overwhelmed, take a break with a mental health **#SNACK.**

STOP - Force yourself to stop for a minute or two to take a breath. Whenever we stop something, we get to begin again with a new attitude. We can give ourselves a restart like this whenever we want.

NOTICE - Notice what is going on inside you and what are the feelings, sensations, and thoughts.

ACCEPT- Whatever you're struggling with is only made worse if you don't accept it fully. Adding judgments or imposing 'should's' on the situation make for more suffering.

CURIOSITY - Rather than judge or bully yourself, try and shift into some curiosity about what you're experiencing and why.

KINDNESS - Treating ourselves with anything but kindness will only make things worse. Our well-being depends on the way we treat ourselves.

WEEKLY

HAPPY   What am I grateful for the most this week?

INTENT   What is my personal intention this week?

MINDFUL   In what areas can I be more mindful in?

HAPPY

INTENT

MINDFUL

PRIORITIES FOR THIS WEEK:

How different would your life be if all criticism, internal and external were removed from you and your relationships?

#SNACK

How can you be more compassionate to yourself? What would that look like?

S T U C K

SHARE IT

TRUTH

UNDERSTAND

KICK THE FEELS

We all get stuck sometimes, whether it's at school or in relationships. Knowing what to do once we are stuck defines our success or failure in the matter. Here's a handy acronym to give you some pointers towards finding your way out.

SHARE IT - Being stuck alone with a problem or situation is very different from being stuck and talking about it with someone you trust. Don't keep it to yourself!

TRUTH - Separate the truth from what you're adding to it. "I failed my Biology exam" is very different from "I failed my Biology exam, and I am so stupid." The latter part is an addition that doesn't help.

UNDERSTAND - Understand what you're feeling as being separate from the hard facts. Failing an exam is a fact, and any feelings of frustration and disappointment are separate.

CAPTIVATE - Captivate the facts and focus on what you can do about them. If you failed an exam, can you retake it? Can you make up for it with extra credit?

KICK THE FEELS - After you've understood your feelings and expressed them, kick them to the curb! They are just a reaction to an event and might not be serving you if you hold onto them.

WEEKLY

WHO   Who can I help this week?

WHAT   What are three things I can do this week to move forward?

HELP   Who is the ideal person to help me if I am stuck?

WHO

WHAT

HELP

PRIORITIES FOR THIS WEEK:

Who can you turn to for help when you are stuck?
What could you *never* ask for help about?

#STUCK

What are some of the ways that your brain and thinking patterns can make things even worse when you're stuck? What are some alternatives for next time?

#IMPROVE

BIG FEELINGS

IMAGERY

MEANING

PRAYER

RELAXATION

ONE THING

VACATE

ENCOURAGE

#IMPROVE is another Dialectical Behavioral Therapy skill used to help improve the moment when you are struggling with big feelings.

IMAGERY - Using our imagination to picture something soothing or a favorite place can lower the intensity of our feelings.

MEANING - Thinking of the important things in your life, what your goals are or how you've got through tough times before can help soothe you.

PRAYER - Use your spirituality or religion, or just be mindful to shift the direction of your thoughts.

RELAXATION- Practicing a calming routine or deep breathing activity will lower agitation in our body.

ONE THING - Focus on one thing in the moment, your feet on the ground, or the task you're currently in the middle of. Slow your thoughts down.

VACATE - Take a break if you can, go for a walk, and change the scenery.

ENCOURAGE - Make helpful positive statements to yourself or others if you notice your thoughts are judgemental or negative.

WEEKLY

WIN   What were the big wins for you from the previous week?

GROWTH   What is your growth edge- these are areas that you could do better in?

GOAL   What are the main goals of the week ahead?

WIN

GROWTH

GOAL

PRIORITIES FOR THIS WEEK:

Which is worse, failing or never trying?

#IMPROVE

What are you avoiding most in life?

#HOPE

HOLD SPACE

OWN FEELINGS

PROBLEM SOLVE

EMPATHIZE

FRIENDS

My People Patterns

When someone we love is upset, it would be natural to want to help them by fixing things or helping them. This usually is how we want to express care and show support for someone. However, getting mixed up in someone else's problems might backfire and is not always the best action. Here's what therapists recommend:

HOLD SPACE - this is a therapist-y way of saying, let someone feel what they are feeling, without trying to change it, but by remaining supportive.

OWN YOUR FEELINGS - you may be having your own feelings, either because someone you love is upset or because you're involved in the situation too. Owning your feelings means understanding where your reaction is coming from.

PROBLEM SOLVE TOGETHER - Rather than offer solutions like 'I'll go get a teacher", start a discussion about the answer. "How can I help?" or "What do you think we can do together."

EMPATHIZE - Put yourself in the other person's shoes and try to understand what they are reacting to. It feels good when someone 'gets' your feelings.

WEEKLY

MORE   What do I need more help with or more of this week?

PRIDE   What could I do this week that will make me feel proud?

HAPPY   Who do I feel grateful for this week, and why?

GOAL

BLOCK

VISION

PRIORITIES FOR THIS WEEK:

How do you normally react when someone you care about is upset? Do you care-take or give them space?

#HOPE

How do you know your friends care about you? When did you feel the most supported by them?

#DREAM

DEDICATION

RESPONSIBILITY

EDUCATION

ATTITUDE

MOTIVATION

MOTIVATION

My People Patterns

If you've ever been told to visualize something you want to make come true, you've probably also been told to 'dream big' or 'go for your dreams.' There's a bit more to do to make your dreams come true, but these sayings, combined with the **#DREAM** acronym, are aimed at giving you the confidence and belief that you absolutely CAN make anything possible.

"The future belongs to those who believe in the beauty of their dreams." – Eleanor Roosevelt

The more feelings and creativity you put into your vision of your future, the more likely you are to see it become real; our feelings about the image will drive us forward to take steps to make them real.

WEEKLY

GOAL What are my goals for this week?

BLOCKS What is it about me that gets in the way of me reaching my goals?

VISION What could I do differently when and if I run into my blocks?

GOAL

BLOCK

VISION

PRIORITIES FOR THIS WEEK:

What is the one job, cause, or activity that could get you out of bed happily for the rest of your life?

#DREAM

What would you say is one thing you'd like to change in the world?

#SPACE

SORT

PURGE

ACTUALIZE

CONTAINERIZE

EQUALIZE

When we are anxious and stressed, we are most likely to shift into an autopilot mode of business. Sometimes this feels like our brains are crowded with thoughts, and we rush frantically to do all the things we need to without actually getting things done well. This tool will help declutter and give **#SPACE**

SORT - sort your thoughts and separate facts, feelings, and judgments

PURGE - set aside any unhelpful thoughts

ACTUALIZE - what is *actually* needed to resolve this, versus being right.

CONTAINERIZE - don't get distracted or off-topic

EQUALIZE - restore balance

WEEKLY

HAPPY   What am I grateful for the most this week?

INTENT   What is my personal intention this week?

MINDFUL   In what areas can I be more mindful in?

AWESOME

CONTENT

GROWTH

PRIORITIES FOR THIS WEEK:

When you are at your most stressed, what happens to your thinking?
Does it get cluttered or in need of #SPACE?

#SPACE

What do you see on your schedule that makes your stress levels go through the roof? What could you remove and why?

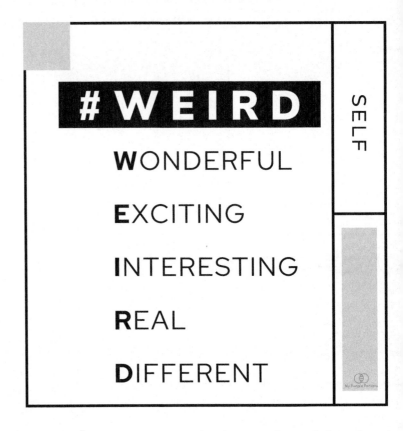

#WEIRD

WONDERFUL

EXCITING

INTERESTING

REAL

DIFFERENT

SELF

It's often more challenging for us to see what's good or right about ourselves than it is to see what's wrong or needs to change. Even thinking about any positive traits they might have, makes some people very anxious. Other people have a problem believing in themselves too much which can be seen as vain or arrogant.

A healthy middle ground is self-appreciation - it's when we can acknowledge that all people have strengths and weaknesses. As just another person on this planet. we are no different. If we allow ourselves to revel in our positive traits while also understanding there's room for improvement, we can generate a healthy and balanced self-image.

We can be both **#WEIRD** and wonderful because we are all unique creatures.

WEEKLY

LEARN   What did I learn about myself this week?

PRIDE   What do I feel good about doing or accomplishing this week?

CURIOUS   What topics or areas do I find myself curious about knowing more of?

LEARN

PRIDE

CURIOUS

PRIORITIES FOR THIS WEEK:

Are the things you don't like about yourself really true? Or do you just believe that they are true?

#WEIRD

Do you have any limiting beliefs that prevent you from showing yourself more self-love and self-appreciation?

#PAWS

PAUSE & THINK

ALWAYS BREATHE

WALK AWAY

SOLVE or RESOLVE

The worst thing we can do when we're angry at someone is to keep the conversation going for longer than it needs to. When we're dysregulated and mad, the mature parts of our brain we need to be active are not online, so it's doubtful anything good will come from a heated exchange.

PAUSE AND THINK - this is probably the most challenging step, especially when we're fuming mad. Consider the consequences of continuing the disagreement and what you want in the long term.

ALWAYS BREATHE - take two deep breaths before you say anything; this one simple thing could make a difference in what happens next.

WALK AWAY - if you're still mad after pausing and breathing, it's ok to walk away. I suggest you tell the other person that you need a few minutes to calm down. Otherwise, it might look like you're storming off.

SOLVE OR RESOLVE - Once calmer, go back and see if you can talk calmly about the problem or issue. Sometimes it's good to start with a question like, "Ok; I want to work this out. Can we think about how we might resolve this?"

WEEKLY

WHO — Which of my relationships, if any, should I look to improve?

HOW — Can I do or say anything different around this person?

SHIFT — What is one thing I like or admire about someone I have difficulty with?

AWESOME

CONTENT

GROWTH

PRIORITIES FOR THIS WEEK:

How does your family deal with anger? Is there anything in the way they deal with conflict you want to keep or change?

#PAWS

How long can you stay angry at someone or something before it starts bothering you? How do you know when it's impacting your life?

#RAIN

RECOGNIZE

ALLOW

INVESTIGATE

NON-IDENTIFICATION

#RAIN is an acronym developed by Michelle McDonald, a mindfulness teacher who created this technique to help us become more aware of what we are feeling and to lean into our emotions, even when we might instead run from them.

RECOGNIZE - rather than react to a feeling, try to recognize that you are reacting to something; perhaps it's irritation at how someone is talking to you.

ALLOW and ACCEPT that this feeling is coming up; when we act too fast to change a feeling or judge it, we add to our suffering.

INVESTIGATE - try and adopt a stance of curiosity, exploring why you have the reaction you are - is it because you're tired or stressed? Explore why you are having the reaction you are.

NON-IDENTIFICATION - you are not your feelings! Try to disentangle yourself from the experience, knowing that feelings come and go and are not permanent.

WEEKLY

WIN What were the big wins for you from the previous week?

GROWTH What is your growth edge– these are areas that you could do better in?

GOAL What are the main goals of the week ahead?

WIN

GROWTH

GOAL

PRIORITIES FOR THIS WEEK:

What feelings are you most likely to run away from?

#RAIN

In what situations are you most likely to need to use this tool?

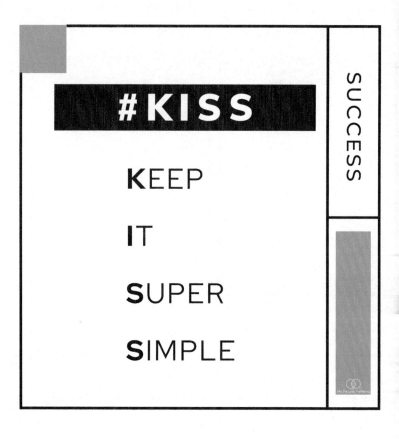

#KISS

KEEP

IT

SUPER

SIMPLE

SUCCESS

Some of us tend to add more to our lives, another page to the essay we're writing, or one more skincare product to the routine. While deciding to add more may feel good at the moment, sometimes less is more, particularly if we want to be less anxious.

> **"I have just three things to teach: simplicity, patience, compassion. These three are your greatest treasures."**
> ~Lao-Tze

If you miss someone .... call them
If you have questions .... ask
If you want to be understood. ... explain
If you like someone.... tell them

WEEKLY

AWESOME   What totally lit me up and excited me?

CONTENT   What am I satisfied with just the way it is?

GROWTH   In what area should I focus on improving in this week?

AWESOME

CONTENT

GROWTH

PRIORITIES FOR THIS WEEK:

In what areas of your life do you tend
to add more to, only to regret it later?

K I S S

How does the amount of information you're exposed to
impact your stress levels? School, advertising, social media?

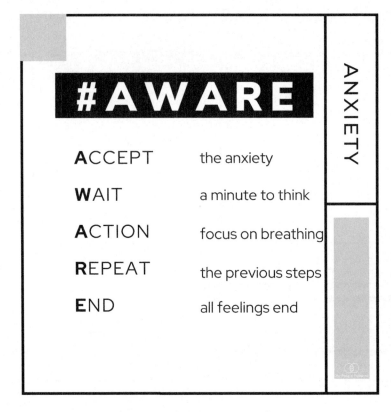

#AWARE

ANXIETY

ACCEPT	the anxiety
WAIT	a minute to think
ACTION	focus on breathing
REPEAT	the previous steps
END	all feelings end

The **#AWARE** approach to anxiety is helpful for anyone who has anxiety symptoms like overwhelming nervousness and worry. These symptoms can often have debilitating effects, including an inability to focus at work or school. Some individuals may altogether avoid interacting with other people, including friends or family members, to try and avoid experiencing panic attacks.

ACCEPT & ACKNOWLEDGE Accepting your feelings is the first step, don't try and convince yourself you're not anxious when you are! It only makes it worse.

WAIT& WATCH -Take a minute to breathe and try and think; this is better than distracting yourself or going 'outside' yourself to avoid things.

ACTIONS - make yourself comfortable, take deep breaths, journal, try a guided meditation

REPEAT - Sometimes, your anxiety will come back after you calm down, so you may have to repeat these steps.

END - All feelings pass, so remind yourself that this will pass.

WEEKLY

HAPPY What am I grateful for the most this week?

INTENT What is my personal intention this week?

MINDFUL In what areas can I be more mindful in?

HAPPY

INTENT

MINDFUL

PRIORITIES FOR THIS WEEK:

What is a way your anxiety has held you back recently?

#AWARE

Describe a time when you felt free from anxiety. Where were you? What were you doing? What about that memory allowed you to not feel anxiety?

> "To know thyself is the beginning of wisdom."
>
> - Socrates

#LEARN

Listen

Enter open-minded

Always be curious

Respect self and others

Never make excuses

SELF

ROUND ONE:

Think of a problem you're currently having and ask yourself these questions:

What's wrong with me?
What's wrong with them?
Whose fault is it?
Why does this always happen?

ROUND TWO:

Now think of the same problem and ask yourself these questions:

What do I appreciate about myself?
What do I appreciate about them?
What can I learn from this?
What are the best steps forward?

At the end of each round, ask yourself, what did you notice, what did you feel, and where did your thoughts go?

Whenever I've done this with clients, they look different at the end of each set of questions, more alert, upright, and open at the end of round two. When you ask yourself the right questions, you enter a 'learning' state of mind, it feels different, there are more opportunities, and as a result, there are often more opportunities and possibilities.

WEEKLY

LEARN   What did I learn about myself this week?

PRIDE   What do I feel good about doing or accomplishing this week?

CURIOUS   What topics or areas do I find myself curious about knowing more of?

LEARN

PRIDE

CURIOUS

PRIORITIES FOR THIS WEEK:

What are your thinking patterns normally like? Those in Round One – more judgemental, or those in Round Two?

#LEARN

What do you think life is teaching you right now? What can you learn about yourself or the world with whatever is going on?

#THINK

Is it... **T**ruthful?

Helpful?

Insightful?

Necessary?

Kind?

Actions might speak louder than words, but we often underestimate the power of our words. What we say or write can create beautiful new relationships and, at the same time, really hurt other people. When you watch your words, you are actively caring for the people around you; and choosing what to say with more wisdom can only positively impact all your relationships.

The words we use internally when we talk to ourselves are just as important as the ones we use to communicate with friends and family, so ask yourself::

Is it Truthful?
Is it Helpful?
Is it Insightful?
Is it Necessary?
Is it Kind?

WEEKLY

MORE — What do I need more help with or more of this week?

PRIDE — What could I do this week that will make me feel proud?

HAPPY — Who do I feel grateful for this week, and why?

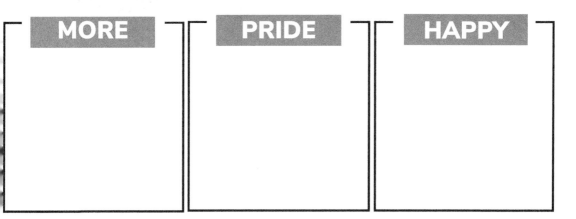

MORE

PRIDE

HAPPY

PRIORITIES FOR THIS WEEK:

Have you ever said something and later regretted it? What did you say and why did you regret it?

#THINK

In what way do you need to change the way you speak to yourself to a more compassionate, understanding dialogue?

#START

SCHEDULE

THE

ACTION

REQUIRED

TODAY

My People Patterns

When we are faced with feelings of overwhelm or are battling some procrastination, it's easy to avoid, hide, or just get sucked into a YouTube wormhole. We tend to avoid uncertainty or things we don't understand and only get things done when there's so much pressure; the only option is to get it done.

A more manageable alternative is to break the task or project down into small parts and then take one action at a time. In the business world, executives are trained to schedule the first meeting on a project, even if they have no idea what they are doing. Scheduling the first meeting or taking the first step signals to our brain that we are going to make things happen and are unafraid of the unknown.

WEEKLY

GOAL — What are my goals for this week?

BLOCKS — What is it about me that gets in the way of me reaching my goals?

VISION — What could I do differently when and if I run into my blocks?

GOAL

BLOCK

VISION

PRIORITIES FOR THIS WEEK:

What are you most likely to procrastinate doing? Why? (Is it because you hate doing it, or because you don't know how?)

#START

Sometimes you can beat procrastination by asking yourself: What is one thing I can do to get started, and when?

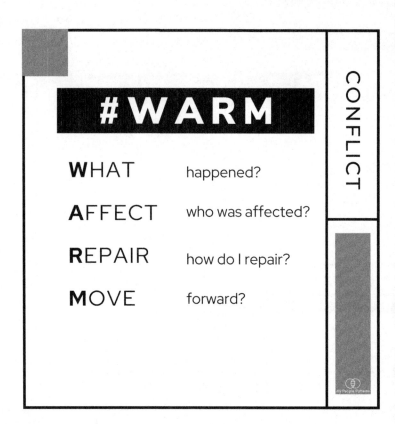

#WARM

WHAT   happened?

AFFECT   who was affected?

REPAIR   how do I repair?

MOVE   forward?

CONFLICT

Conflict and misunderstandings are an inevitable part of being in any type of relationship, but learning how to navigate tricky times with people we care about is challenging. It's helpful to remember to keep the conversation **#WARM** when dealing with conflict.

WHAT HAPPENED

Is this normal? A one-off event or does it happen often
What was I thinking about at the time?
What am I thinking about after the conflict?

AFFECT -

Who was affected by what happened?
Was whatever happened fair to them?
Was it the 'right' thing?

REPAIR

What might the other person be feeling?
What do I need to do to repair the relationship?

MOVE FORWARD

How can we make sure this doesn't happen again?
What happens if it does happen again?

WEEKLY

WHO   Which of my relationships, if any, should I look to improve?

HOW   Can I do or say anything different around this person?

SHIFT   What is one thing I like or admire about someone I have difficulty with?

AWESOME

CONTENT

GROWTH

PRIORITIES FOR THIS WEEK:

Who is the person you are most angry with?

W A R M

What do you feel underneath your anger?

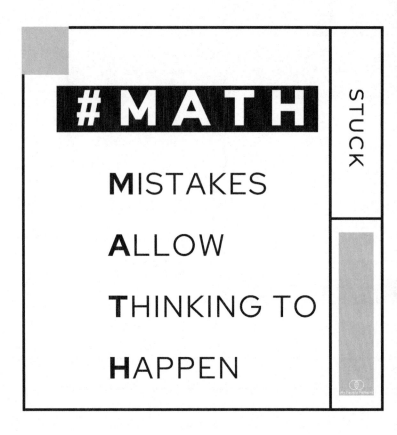

#MATH

MISTAKES

ALLOW

THINKING TO

HAPPEN

We all trip up, make mistakes, screw things up, and have big feelings about such events. As if that is not enough, we continue to pile on negative emotions by beating ourselves up! Doing so adds even more suffering and stress to an already uncomfortable experience.

Sometimes, we need to decide not to dwell on some of our blunders and move on. Other times there can be a silver lining in our mistakes if we can stop screaming at ourselves for making a mistake in the first place.

We have to give ourselves a little grace for the blunder, but then we need to acknowledge any of the opportunities and growth we've made since our last mistake. The only comparison we should be making is to ourselves.

WEEKLY

WHO   Who can I help this week?

WHAT   What are three things I can do this week to move forward?

HELP   Who is the ideal person to help me if I am stuck?

WHO

WHAT

HELP

PRIORITIES FOR THIS WEEK:

Think of the last time you made a mistake or got rejected– what can you learn about yourself, or the problem?

M A T H

How much do you let what others think about you influence your feelings around success and failure?

#ACCEPTS

ACTIVITIES

CONTRIBUTING

COMPARISONS

EMOTIONS

PUSHING AWAY

THOUGHTS

SENSATIONS

#ACCEPTS is a tool from DBT that teaches us to deal with challenging or uncomfortable feelings. It's best used when it's not possible to change a situation.

ACTIVITIES - Get physical with chores, exercise, or listening to music - distract yourself from the feeling.

CONTRIBUTING - helping other people is a guaranteed way to get out of our own heads and distract from big feelings.

COMPARISONS - If you compare the current situation to an even worse situation, we can sometimes get perspective which can shift our moods.

EMOTIONS - Act in an opposite way from what you're feeling, so if you are sad, try dancing to your favorite song. Go to a calm place if you're feeling anxious.

PUSHING AWAY - Push away any negative thoughts, sometimes you can write them out and then rip the page up.

THOUGHTS - put new thoughts into your head to overcrowd the negative thoughts- something like a puzzle or a video game might work.

SENSATIONS - Use physical sensations like cold water or a warm bath to change your mood.

WEEKLY

WIN — What were the big wins for you from the previous week?

GROWTH — What is your growth edge- these are areas that you could do better in?

GOAL — What are the main goals of the week ahead?

WIN

GROWTH

GOAL

PRIORITIES FOR THIS WEEK:

What negative feelings do you struggle to deal with? Guilt, shame, sadness, fear and anger are common responses.

#ACCEPTS

What do you find effective in changing your feelings? What will you try next time your mood changes to a big feeling?

#RICH

REALIZING

I

CREATE

HAPPINESS

A study from the University of Illinois found that people who earn the most millions of dollars a year are only a tiny bit happier than the average person who works for them. Another study from the University of California found that genetics only account for about 50% of how happy a person is. So... how do you create your happiness?

WEEKLY

AWESOME   What totally lit me up and excited me?

CONTENT   What am I satisfied with just the way it is?

GROWTH   In what area should I focus on improving in this week?

AWESOME

CONTENT

GROWTH

PRIORITIES FOR THIS WEEK:

What are the top five things in your life that you love and that make you happy?

Do you need more or less of them in your life?

R I C H

What do you need to change in order to be happy?

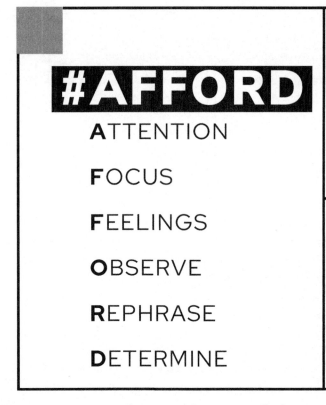

#AFFORD

ATTENTION

FOCUS

FEELINGS

OBSERVE

REPHRASE

DETERMINE

It feels SO good when someone you know and trust really listens to you, although you might only know this through contrast because it feels really annoying when someone doesn't listen to you. **#AFFORD** is a tool that helps us remember how to listen in all the ways that feel good to the person talking.

ATTENTION - giving someone your full attention should be the only thing you're doing. Put the phone down and close the book!

FOCUS - I often tell people to listen as if they have an exam on the topic the speaker is discussing. It should be quite tiring to listen fully.

FEELINGS - try and identify what feelings the person has about what they are discussing. Are they angry, or ... are they angry because they are hurt?

OBSERVE - one way to tell what the person is feeling is by observing their body language. It might give you more clues.

REPHRASE - check with the speaker to see if you're fully getting it by repeating some of it, 'So wait, this all was on Saturday night *after* the movie ended?'

DETERMINE - If you're not sure, ask for more information. 'I think I need to know more about what happened on the way to the theater'.

WEEKLY

MORE   What do I need more help with or more of this week?

PRIDE   What could I do this week that will make me feel proud?

HAPPY   Who do I feel grateful for this week, and why?

MORE

PRIDE

HAPPY

PRIORITIES FOR THIS WEEK:

What qualities do you have that make you a good friend? Which would you like to improve on?

#AFFORD

What qualities do you look for in a friendship? What is important to you about the people you're friends with?

#REDUCE

		ANXIETY
REMINDER	Feelings pass	
ENFORCE	Boundaries	
DROP	Excess	
USE	Coping Skills	
CONTACT	Support team	
EVALUATE	Your well-being	

#REDUCE is an acronym that is useful to remember when we need to manage our stress levels, but even more so when we're prone to anxiety.

The **#REDUCE** acronym is a way to remember some tips to help you lower stress levels as quickly as you can

REMIND - yourself that it's ok to feel whatever you are feeling, don't judge your feelings, they just happen.

ENFORCE -your personal boundaries - clearly state your needs and limits

DROP - drop anything from your life that is not immediately important

USE - your coping skills

CONTACT - your support people

EVALUATE - your well-being on a daily basis and ask for more help when and if needed.

WEEKLY

HAPPY What am I grateful for the most this week?

INTENT What is my personal intention this week?

MINDFUL In what areas can I be more mindful in?

HAPPY

INTENT

MINDFUL

PRIORITIES FOR THIS WEEK:

What does your support system look like? Who can you turn to for help? Who can you turn to who will listen?

#REDUCE

Write out your coping skills to deal with anxiety, and consider this page to be your anxiety toolkit. Next time you're feeling anxious, pick one of the things to from this.

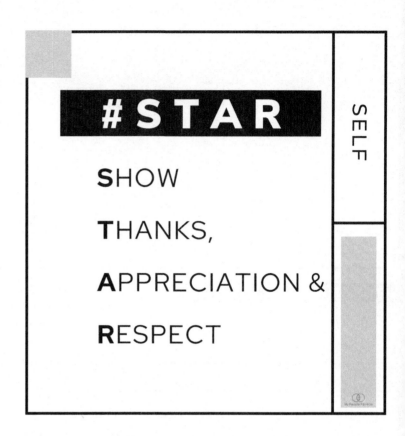

#STAR

SHOW

THANKS,

APPRECIATION &

RESPECT

SELF

In the world of Positive Psychology, the branch of psychology that focuses on well-being and happiness, gratitude is consistently associated in studies with higher levels of well-being and contentment.

Research shows that allowing ourselves to feel thankful towards someone or something changes our inner world in that we feel lighter or more content. When our inner world changes, we can change our outer world, too; it's as if we radiate positivity when we focus on gratitude as a habit.

LEARN   What did I learn about myself this week?

PRIDE   What do I feel good about doing or accomplishing this week?

CURIOUS   What topics or areas do I find myself curious about knowing more of?

LEARN

PRIDE

CURIOUS

PRIORITIES FOR THIS WEEK:

Who in your life made you laugh, smile, or feel good about yourself in the last two weeks? As you write the list, remember the feelings – this is called 'savoring'.

S T A R

How do you normally express gratitude to people? Can you think of anyone on this list that would be easy to share some of your gratitude with? How would you do it?

#PAINS

POSITIVE

ATTITUDE

IN

NEGATIVE

SITUATIONS

STUCK

In Cognitive Behavioral Therapy, we learn that our thoughts produce our feelings. If you think about something sad, you will inevitably start feeling sad. Ultimately how we feel impacts our behaviors; for better or worse, when you feel sad, you're probably much less likely to want to go out and meet friends. Falling down a negative thoughts and feelings spiral happens to everyone once in a while, so learning to catch yourself from slipping down that slope is a very important life skill. Learning the power of positive thinking helps you stay positive even amid difficulties and is invaluable in leading a healthy lifestyle.

However, suppose we only focus on the positive aspects and deny our authentic and valid feelings about whatever challenges we face? In that case, it leans towards 'toxic positivity' or a 'spiritual bypass.'

The real trick to success is holding our feelings without being sucked too far into them while also maintaining a positive or neutral mindset. This is hard work... but not impossible.

WEEKLY

WHO — Who can I help this week?

WHAT — What are three things I can do this week to move forward?

HELP — Who is the ideal person to help me if I am stuck?

WHO

WHAT

HELP

PRIORITIES FOR THIS WEEK:

How long does it usually take you to bounce back from failure?

#PAINS

How often do you tell yourself "I can't"?

#RELAX

RELEASE

EVERY

LITTLE

ANNOYING

EXPERIENCE

MOTIVATION

My People Pattern

Sometimes our stress levels come from holding onto things that do not serve us, old relationships, negative memories, or even our guilt and shame. Often we've been holding onto these things for so long that they are comforting or at least relatively familiar. Not holding onto them would be a new feeling, and we tend to avoid the unfamiliar, so we hold onto things.

We gain a sense of inner freedom when we let go of things holding us down or no longer serving us. When are not so mentally involved in things from the past or future outcomes and are content to be in the here and now.

This freedom is available to anyone, often, people go to therapy to relieve themselves of such burdens, but journalling is just as effective.

WEEKLY

GOAL What are my goals for this week?

BLOCKS What is it about me that gets in the way of me reaching my goals?

VISION What could I do differently when and if I run into my blocks?

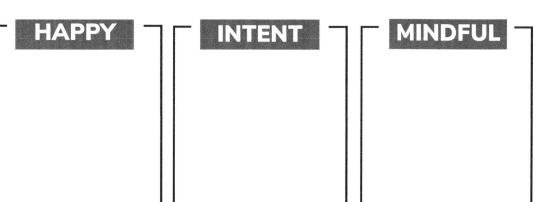

HAPPY

INTENT

MINDFUL

PRIORITIES FOR THIS WEEK:

Write down two memories that cause you to be unhappy or unfilled that you might want to let go of.

#RELAX

What stops you from letting go of these memories? What do you gain out of holding onto them?

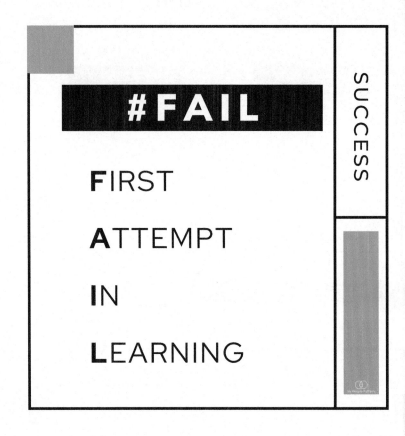

#FAIL

FIRST

ATTEMPT

IN

LEARNING

SUCCESS

Trying to reframe failure or disappointment as an opportunity to grow stronger is easily said and often offered to us as a way to cheer us up. Turning something around like this is much more challenging. However, shifting our mindset and negative self-talk is the most productive way of handling life when you get given a whole bunch of lemons.

EVERYONE FAILS

Let's keep this real, everyone fails. J.K. Rowling got turned down by 12 different publishers. Howard Schultz, got turned down 242 times for a business loan to start Starbucks. The idea of opening a theme park got rejected 302 times before someone said to 'yes' to building Disneyland.

WEEKLY

AWESOME — What totally lit me up and excited me?

CONTENT — What am I satisfied with just the way it is?

GROWTH — In what area should I focus on improving in this week?

AWESOME

CONTENT

GROWTH

PRIORITIES FOR THIS WEEK:

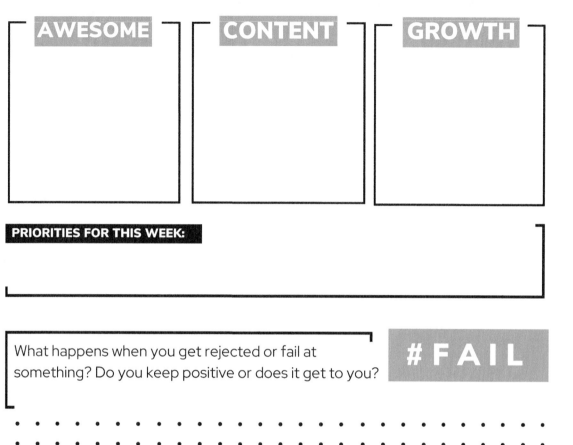

What happens when you get rejected or fail at something? Do you keep positive or does it get to you?

#FAIL

Think of the last time you failed or got rejected, how can you re-write or reframe the story you tell yourself about it?

#STOP

STOP

TAKE A STEP BACK

OBSERVE

PROCEED MINDFULLY

This is a classic Dialectical Behavioral Therapy Skills (DBT) that has been adapted from the original by Marsha Linehan. Navy Seals use an incredibly similar protocol in distressful situations in which emotional reactivity could be fatal.

STOP - don't react, if appropriate, don't move. Your body and feelings may try to act reactively, so stay in control.

TAKE A STEP BACK - if you can create some space between you and the situation, either physically or emotionally, by taking a time out.

OBSERVE - What are your feelings and thoughts? What are others saying or doing?

PROCEED MANUALLY - Be aware of the situation, others, and your feelings. When emotions run high, there can be a lot of volatility, so keep your goals and values in mind. Remind yourself of consequences.

WEEKLY

WHO   Which of my relationships, if any, should I look to improve?

HOW   Can I do or say anything different around this person?

SHIFT   What is one thing I like or admire about someone I have difficulty with?

WIN

GROWTH

GOAL

PRIORITIES FOR THIS WEEK:

When you feel overwhelmed, how do you normally respond? What could you do differently next time?

#STOP

When you are angry with someone, how do you deal with it? What would be a better way of resolving disagreements?

#PAUSE

PAY ATTENTION

ASSESS

UNDERSTAND

SET BOUNDARIES

EMPATHIZE

#PAUSE is an acronym for a tool used to de-escalate big feelings and is particularly useful for anger, but can be applied to other feelings.

PAY ATTENTION - to my body, thoughts, and feelings. Know what the sensations and thoughts are that lead up to big emotions.

ASSESS - what is activating you? What feelings are coming up? Do you feel misunderstood or unheard? Hurt or scared?

UNDERSTAND - the roots of the feeling. Have boundaries been crossed, are values being challenged, and is a power struggle occurring that causes fear or anger?

SET BOUNDARIES - if you cannot be present with the feelings coming up, step away. Set boundaries of a time out until you are more grounded.

EMPATHIZE - with those involved. How are other people experiencing you? How do your actions impact others? What are other people trying to express?

WEEKLY

WIN What were the big wins for you from the previous week?

GROWTH What is your growth edge- these are areas that you could do better in?

GOAL What are the main goals of the week ahead?

WIN

GROWTH

GOAL

PRIORITIES FOR THIS WEEK:

Do you have an accurate idea of what triggers big feelings inside you? Is it anger? Fear? Being misunderstood?

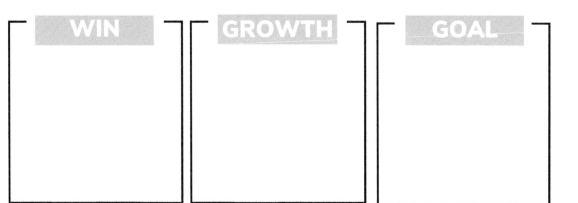

#PAUSE

Who is it that you really need to forgive?

#FEAR

FOCUS

EXPOSE

APPROACH

REHEARSE

ANXIETY

Fear and anxiety can cripple us at times and put us in a state of paralysis that erodes our ability to think clearly and make the best possible decisions. This acronym reminds us that fear is often distorted in our thinking.

FOCUS - on the present, don't freak out. Lots of research from Mindfulness-Based Cognitive Therapy can lower our anxiety by changing the focus to the here and now.

EXPOSE - We often try to escape feelings of fear and anxiety, but it's more beneficial to lean into our experience. This way, we can build our tolerance for distressful situations in small increments.

APPROACH - the tendency to avoid or procrastinate is often fueled by anxiety, which only grows when we avoid it. Approaching the thing we fear in gradual or incremental ways is shown in studies to be helpful.

REHEARSE - Athletes, actors, public speakers, and dancers all rehearse, yet we seem to forget that we can do the same in other situations we get anxious about.

HAPPY   What am I grateful for the most this week?

INTENT   What is my personal intention this week?

MINDFUL   In what areas can I be more mindful in?

HAPPY

INTENT

MINDFUL

PRIORITIES FOR THIS WEEK:

Where in your body do you feel anxiety? How else do you know if you're anxious?

 # F E A R

When you start to feel anxious, what do you *usually* do about it? And what could you do differently next time you start to worry?

#RESPECT

RECOGNIZE

ELIMINATE

SPEAK

PRACTICE

EARN

CONSIDER

TREAT

SUCCESS

Successful people have a deep respect for the dignity of other people regardless of their position, age or experience. Here's what **#RESPECT** stands for

RECOGNIZE - try to see the potential and value of everyone you meet.

ELIMINATE - things like gossip, talking smack, or badmouthing others.

SPEAK - speak *with* people, not about them, over them, or down to them

PRACTICE empathy to understand others and feel more connected to them

EARN - respect by performing respect-worthy behaviors and by speaking respectfully.

CONSIDER - other people's feelings, needs, and wants as much as your own.

TREAT - everyone with dignity, courtesy, and of course, respect.

WEEKLY

AWESOME   What totally lit me up and excited me?

CONTENT   What am I satisfied with just the way it is?

GROWTH   In what area should I focus on improving in this week?

AWESOME

CONTENT

GROWTH

PRIORITIES FOR THIS WEEK:

Do you respect yourself enough? How do you disrespect yourself? (physically, mentally, or socially)

#RESPECT

Who do you respect the most? Who do you respect the least? Why these people and what is different about them?

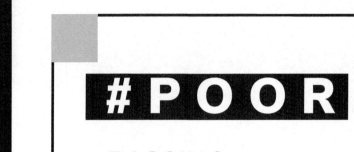

P O O R

PASSING

OVER

OPPORTUNITIES

REPEATEDLY

STUCK

Opportunities come in all shapes and sizes, and it's probably true to say that there's an unequal distribution of opportunities to everyone. Nevertheless, opportunities come our way often, and being open and unafraid to take them makes a massive difference over one's life.

"Life opens up opportunities to you, and you either take them, or you stay afraid of taking them"
Jim Carey

Being afraid of taking opportunities means we stay in our comfort zone and don't get the chance to grow and expand ourselves.

WEEKLY

WHO   Who can I help this week?

WHAT   What are three things I can do this week to move forward?

HELP   Who is the ideal person to help me if I am stuck?

WHO

WHAT

HELP

PRIORITIES FOR THIS WEEK:

If you knew you couldn't fail, what would you say 'yes' to doing?

P O O R

What holds you back from taking opportunities that come your way?

#VITALS

Values

Interests

Temperament

Around The Clock Activities

Life Goals

Strengths

SELF

#VITALS represents six building blocks of your identity or sense of self, which are the key to self-esteem and success. Learning about the aspects of our identity often results in greater happiness, less internal conflict, and the ability to set better boundaries.

VALUES -research shows us that knowing our values helps us feel more secure and to make better decisions; values are like a compass as we navigate life.

INTERESTS - having interests in things makes life more vibrant and exciting, so understanding what lights up our curiosity is vital to us all.

TEMPERAMENT - These are the preferences we seem to be born with, like being an introvert or extravert, if you're more spontaneous or prefer to plan.

ACTIVITIES - This refers to your biorhythms, which are essential to understand. Are you a morning person or a night owl? What time of day can you concentrate the best?

LIFE GOALS - If you could do anything in the world, what would it be and why? The answers to these questions may be part of your identity and self-understanding

STRENGTHS - At the core of self-confidence is knowing what you're good at which can include not only abilities, skills, and talents but also character strengths such as loyalty or creativity.

WEEKLY

LEARN   What did I learn about myself this week?

PRIDE   What do I feel good about doing or accomplishing this week?

CURIOUS   What topics or areas do I find myself curious about knowing more of?

LEARN

PRIDE

CURIOUS

PRIORITIES FOR THIS WEEK:

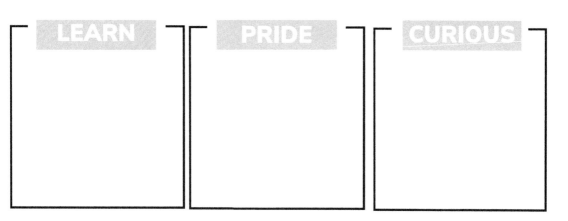

What have been the three most meaningful events of your life? These can sometimes reveal our values.

#VITALS

What do you consider to be your strengths? If you could ask four people what *they* think your strengths are, what would they say?

#LEAF

LISTEN

EMPATHIZE

APOLOGIZE

FIX

CONFLICT

We all know how it feels to be on the receiving end of a lousy apology. You know, the type where they apologize for your feelings and not what they actually did? Here's how to apologize correctly using **#LEAF** tool.

LISTEN - Let the person speak fully, don't rush to get the 'I'm sorry' part done, part of a good apology is to really understand the other person.

EMPATHIZE - Put yourself in the other person's shoes, and understand where they are coming from. This makes the whole process easier for you and feels better for them This may require you to be the bigger person.

APOLOGIZE - Whether you've done something on purpose or not is irrelevant, you have to acknowledge that something you did or said has hurt someone. Don't apologize for how they feel!

FIX - The last step in this is to let the other person know what, if anything, you are going to do to fix the problem or make sure it doesn't happen again.

WEEKLY

WHO   Which of my relationships, if any, should I look to improve?

HOW   Can I do or say anything different around this person?

SHIFT   What is one thing I like or admire about someone I have difficulty with?

AWESOME

CONTENT

GROWTH

PRIORITIES FOR THIS WEEK:

Are there people in your life you have yet to forgive or will never forgive? If so who and why?

#LEAF

What does forgiveness mean to you? Does your definition stop you from forgiving some people?

#SUCCESS

SEE your goal

UNDERSTAND the obstacles

CREATE a vision

CLEAR away doubt

EMBRACE the challenge

STAY on track

SHOW the world YOU

SUCCESS

There is proper and valid scientific research on the art of visualizing your goals, and it comes from the world of social psychology and is backed up with evidence-based data. To create success in your future, putting together a clear vision of what it looks like is a vital first step.

Visualization is used effectively in psychotherapy to help with anxiety and depression, when we create something in our minds, like a blissful beach on a tropical island, our mind reacts to it and our anxiety drops.

EXERCISE - get your vision board going, when physical images are used along with mental images, we are better able to generate feelings that go with it. Our feelings about the goal are what propel us to take action to reach it.

WEEKLY

AWESOME What totally lit me up and excited me?

CONTENT What am I satisfied with just the way it is?

GROWTH In what area should I focus on improving in this week?

AWESOME

CONTENT

GROWTH

PRIORITIES FOR THIS WEEK:

If success has nothing to do with money, what would being successful look like for you?

#SUCCESS

What will it look like in ten years from now? Where will you be living? What will you be doing?

#SELF

ANXIETY

SERENITY

EXERCISE

LOVE

FOOD

Kathleen Hall, the founder of The Stress Institute and Mindful Living Network, uses the acronym **#SELF** to remind her clients how self-care plays a vital role in lowering anxiety symptoms.

SERENITY - this refers to how you can create balance, calm, or peace in your life. Meditation is the obvious 'go-to' here, but listening to a guided visualization for a few minutes or sounds of nature would work.

EXERCISE - has many benefits to our mental wellness and is an integral part of our well-being. Physical activity can energize you in the mornings and provide an outlet for excess energy if you're feeling anxious.

LOVE is as simple as focusing on our relationships and finding time to nurture our relationships. Isolation is linked to all kinds of physical and emotional health issues.

FOOD - what we put into our bodies impacts our health and well-being, being mindful of eating habits and the nutritional value of food is helpful in managing anxiety levels and stress.

WEEKLY

HAPPY   What am I grateful for the most this week?

INTENT   What is my personal intention this week?

MINDFUL   In what areas can I be more mindful in?

HAPPY

INTENT

MINDFUL

PRIORITIES FOR THIS WEEK:

What would an ideal balance of study, friends, family, and play look like for you? How close to reality is that?

#SELF

Which of the four parts of **#S.E.L.F** stands out to you as needing the most attention in your life?

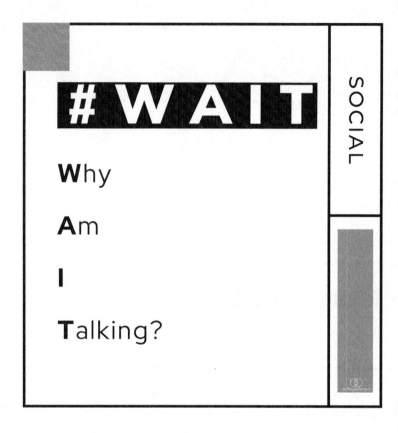

#WAIT

Why

Am

I

Talking?

#WAIT is a brilliant tool to hold onto in any social setting and gives us a chance to pause to consider what we're saying before we say it and to ask ourselves if it's important or helpful to whatever is going on.

"We have two ears and one mouth so that we can listen twice as much as we speak" Aristotle

DARE TO ASK - conversations sometimes get shut down because we don't show enough curiosity. Asking questions to help someone feel understood is a gift.

MASTER THE SILENCE - Just because things go quiet doesn't mean we *have* to fill it. Sometimes silence allows others to explain more and sometimes helps them reveal more.

DON'T COMPETE - topping someone else's story with your own is a surefire way to limit that conversation and turn it into a competition.

WEEKLY

MORE — What do I need more help with or more of this week?

PRIDE — What could I do this week that will make me feel proud?

HAPPY — Who do I feel grateful for this week, and why?

MORE

PRIDE

HAPPY

PRIORITIES FOR THIS WEEK:

How comfortable are you with silence? Does it make you cringe or do you rush to fill it by talking? How could you change this?

#WAIT

In what situations are you most likely to listen, and in what situations are you more likely to talk?

 # R O A R

STUCK

RECOGNIZE

OWN IT

ACCEPT

REFLECT

RECOGNIZE - recognize that you're stuck or something hasn't gone the way you planned. This is normal, part of life, and it sucks. Avoiding this reality or trying to convince yourself otherwise can often backfire.

OWN IT - If we are able to own our 'part' in the situation, if it was a mistake we made or an issue we neglected, we are taking accountability. When we are fully accountable for our part, we can make changes.

ACCEPT- Only when we accept the situation fully as it is and stop trying to deny or blame can we stand a chance of seeing the obstacle in the way.

REFLECT - Perhaps the most important step in growth and success is taking the time to reflect on mistakes, and understanding where you went wrong and what you'd do differently given the chance.

WEEKLY

WHO Who can I help this week?

WHAT What are three things I can do this week to move forward?

HELP Who is the ideal person to help me if I am stuck?

WHO

WHAT

HELP

PRIORITIES FOR THIS WEEK:

Think of a recent mistake or incident that you would rather forget. What can you learn about yourself from it?

#ROAR

What is life trying to teach you right now?

#TIP

TEMPERATURE

INTENSE ACTIVITY

PACE

#TIP is another Dialectical Behavioral Therapy skill made famous by Maciea Linnehan. The skills part of DBT is usually very practical and particularly effective at times.

TEMPERATURE - changing the temperature of your face with cold water has a dramatic impact on your mood. Sometimes this is called Ice-Diving- you fill a big bowl up with water and ice, and as you hold your breath, put your face into the water for 30 seconds.

INTENSE EXERCISE - can rapidly change your mood. If you're feeling depressed, this will enliven your body and release a host of hormones that will lift your spirits. If you're too excited with tension or anxiety, exercise can help calm your mood.

PACE YOUR BREATHING - focus on your breathing and try slowing it down, it has a physiological impact on our emotional state. The out-breath should be longer than the inhale to get maximum impact. 4 seconds in, hold for 7, and out for 8.

WEEKLY

WIN   What were the big wins for you from the previous week?

GROWTH   What is your growth edge- these are areas that you could do better in?

GOAL   What are the main goals of the week ahead?

WIN

GROWTH

GOAL

PRIORITIES FOR THIS WEEK:

What big feelings do you resist having? What big feelings do you have too many of?

#TIP

What normally triggers these feelings and what do you do about them?

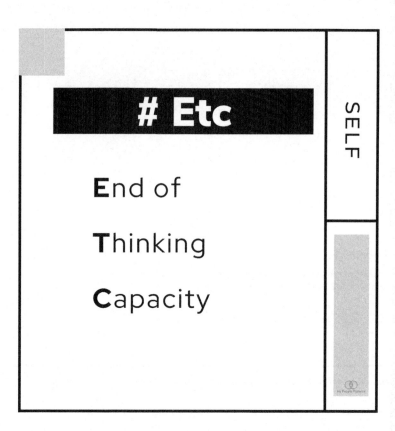

Etc

End of

Thinking

Capacity

We all know that at the end of the day, we need to wind down before bedtime and then have around eight hours of sleep each night. We also all know that no one does this regularly every night, and even if we did, some nights, you just can't sleep. Here are some tips to get some good rest.

> **"At the end of the day remind yourself that you did the best you could today, and that is good enough."**
>
> **Lori Deschene**

1. Read a good book before bed; not too stimulating and not too exciting.
2. Hot showers or hot baths are great if you don't take them right before sleep
3. Remove stimulation - no phones or tablets (sorry!)
4. Creating a ritual around bedtime so that your brain knows it's time to turn off,can be helpful
5. Purge your stress and write your to-do list in a journal or notepad

WEEKLY

LEARN   What did I learn about myself this week?

PRIDE   What do I feel good about doing or accomplishing this week?

CURIOUS What topics or areas do I find myself curious about knowing more of?

LEARN

PRIDE

CURIOUS

PRIORITIES FOR THIS WEEK:

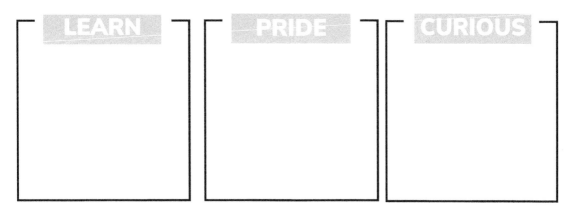

When do you first know that you're at your capacity?
Do the warning signals come on too late?

#Etc

What would be a nighttime ritual you could
create that would be fun and relaxing?

RESOURCES

SEARCH FOR THERAPISTS AND SUPPORT GROUPS

Good Therapy www.goodtherapy.org
Psychology Today www.psychologytoday.com
National Alliance on Mental Illness www.nami.org
Substance Abuse and Mental Health Services Administration www.samhsa.gov
AGPA. - American Group Psychotherapy Association www.AGPA.org

HELP HOTLINES

The National Domestic Violence Hotline 800-799-7233
National Suicide Prevention Lifeline 800-273-8255
National Sexual Assault Hotline 800-656-4673
 TEENLINE (310) 855-4673 TEXT: 839863 https://teenlineonline.org/
Teen Tribe YouthLine (877) 968-8491 https://oregonyouthline.org/
Suicide Prevention Resource Center 1-800-273- TALK (8255) www.sprc.org

RESOURCES FOR PARENTS

Aha! Parenting www.ahaparenting.com
Center for Parent/Youth Understanding https://cpyu.org
Child Development Institute https://childdevelopmentinfo.com
How to Talk So Teens Will Listen and Listen So Teens Will Talk. New York: HarperCollins, 2006.
Focus on the Family www.focusonthefamily.com
HelpGuide www.helpguide.org/home-pages/teen-issues.htm
KidsHealth https://kidshealth.org/en/parents/adolescence.html
ParenTeen Connect https://www.parenteenconnect.org
U.S. Department of Health and Human Services—Office of Population Affairs

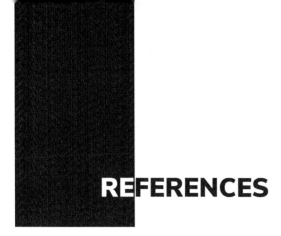

REFERENCES

ACRONYMS

Radović, T., & Manzey, D. (2019). The Impact of a Mnemonic Acronym on Learning and Performing a Procedural Task and Its Resilience Toward Interruptions. Frontiers in Psychology, 10, 2522.

JOURNALING

Mugerwa, S., & Holden, J. D. (2012). Writing therapy: a new tool for general practice? The British Journal of General Practice: The Journal of the Royal College of General Practitioners, 62(605), 661–663.

REFERENCES

#DEARMAN #TIP
#IMPROVE #PAUSE
#ACCEPTS

Linehan, Marsha. (2014. DBT Skills Training Manual, Second Edition. Guilford Publications.

#RAIN

Brach, T. (2020, January 1). RAIN: A Practice of Radical Compassion. Https://www.tarabrach.com/. https://www.tarabrach.com/rain-practice-radical-compassion/

#STIC

Himelstein, S., & Saul, S. (2015). *Mindfulness-based substance abuse treatment for adolescents.* doi:10.4324/9781317607052

#WOOP

Oettingen, G. (2014). Rethinking Positive Thinking: Inside the New Science of Motivation. Current.

#SUCCESS

Cheema, A., & Bagchi, R. (2011). The Effect of Goal Visualization on Goal Pursuit: Implications for Consumers and Managers. Journal of Marketing, 75(2), 109–123.

#SNACK

Naumburg, C. (2016, November 18). How To Take A Mindful Snack. Www.mindful.org. https://www.mindful.org/how-to-take-mindful-snack/

#SELF

Hall, K. (n.d.). Learn S.E.L.F. Care with Dr. Kathleen Hall. Retrieved October 5, 2022, from https://mindfullivingnetwork.com/self-care-with-dr-hall/

#SOS

Finch, H. (2021, April 18). 3-Part Technique to Stop Negative Self-Talk. Https://masteryourmh.com/. https://masteryourmh.com/3-part-technique-to-stop-negative-self-talk/

#VITALS

Selig, M. (2016, March 9). Know Yourself? 6 Specific Ways to Know Who You Are. Psychology Today. https://www.psychologytoday.com/us/blog/changepower/201603/know-yourself-6-specific-ways-know-who-you-are

#THINK

Esposito, L. (2017, March 30). 4 Awesome Acronyms for Anxiety Relief. Psychology Today. https://www.psychologytoday.com/us/blog/anxiety-zen/201703/4-awesome-acronyms-anxiety-relief

#WARM

Thompson, S. (2015, July 15). WARM conversations. Teaching the Teacher. https://traintheteacher.me/2015/07/15/warm-conversations/

#ROAR

Weis, C. (2018, June 8). Cultivating Mindfulness: Teaching Children To Learn From Failure. www.ForTheLoveOfTeachers.com. https://www.fortheloveofteachers.com/cultivating-mindfulness-teaching-children-to-learn-from-failure/

Printed in Great Britain
by Amazon

14930967R00072